W9-AUK-181

Dog Groomer

Earning $50,000–$100,000 with a High School Diploma or Less

Earning $50,000–$100,000
with a High School Diploma or Less

Dog Groomer

CHRISTIE MARLOWE

MASON CREST

Mason Crest
450 Parkway Drive, Suite D
Broomall, PA 19008
www.masoncrest.com

Printed in the United States of America.

First printing
9 8 7 6 5 4 3 2 1

Series ISBN: 978-1-4222-2886-9
ISBN: 978-1-4222-2893-7
ebook ISBN: 978-1-4222-8929-7

Cataloging-in-Publication Data on file with the Library of Congress.

Produced by Vestal Creative Services.
www.vestalcreative.com

Contents

CHAPTER 1
Careers Without College

The nickname, "man's best friend," is more than appropriate considering the long history humans and dogs share. Dogs were the first animals to be domesticated; in other words, they underwent the process where a population of animals or plants is changed through years of breeding in order to emphasize traits that benefit humans. Other examples of domesticated animals include sheep, cattle, pigs, and chickens. Dogs, a domesticated species of the gray wolf, are the most widely kept working, hunting, and pet animal in human history. The dogs

Today's domestic dogs still share a lot of characteristics with their wild wolf cousins. They use similar body language, and both learn quickly and enjoy playing. Scientists believe that these traits are important to dogs' success as a species.

we know and love today are a part of our lives because the gray wolf was domesticated nearly 33 thousand years ago!

Why and how domestication came about is widely debated, but most people are able to agree that the relationship between dogs and humans, especially in the early stages of domestication, was beneficial to both dogs and humans alike. Dogs would have been provided safety from living in human camps, a more reliable food source, and more chances to breed. Humans, on the other hand, benefited from improved sanitation (from dogs cleaning up their food scraps), warmth (from the dogs' bodies and fur), and safety. More important, the presence of a dog would have greatly improved the chances for success when hunting. Former veterinarian and science writer, Dr. Jonica Newby, even suggests that the domestication of dogs is one of the main reasons that humans, as a species, have succeeded as well as they have!

Since being domesticated, the relationship between dogs and humans has come a long way. Over the years they have been bred for herding other domesticated animals, hunting, rodent control, guarding, helping fishermen with nets, detection (such as sniffing for bombs or drugs), and pulling loads (such as sleigh dogs). In recent times, dogs have added to their job description that of assisting individuals with physical or mental disabilities.

Compared to any of these uses, however, the large majority of all dogs are kept as pets. Before World War II, keeping dogs as pets was most often a practice of upper class men and women, but since World War II, the pet population has grown significantly. According to the Humane Society, Americans today own 78.2 million dogs and nearly 40 percent of all households own at least one or more dogs.

And that fact leads to job opportunities! After all, dogs need care. They need medical care from veterinarians. They may need training from professional dog trainers. And they need grooming.

Because dogs are now considered important members of the family, people are more and more willing to pay money for their care.

DOG GROOMER

Dog Groomers

"For many people, their pet is just another member of the family," says Rheya Zimmerman, a veteran dog groomer with over twenty years of experience. "This is especially true for their dogs."

Rheya is right. According to researcher Emma Powers, "The last fifty years have seen dogs increasingly drawn into the home as family members." She even writes that dog owners describe their dogs as "furry children" to emphasize "the time spent caring for dogs." Considering the shared history of dogs and humans and the many ways that we have helped each other grow and survive as species, it's really not all that surprising they've finally been assigned significant roles as members of the family!

"When dogs are considered a luxury, or 'just something nice to have,'" Rheya says, "people are less willing to spend money for their well-being. Today, they are family members—and people will do what it takes to take care of family members."

This is where dog groomers come in. Dog grooming is the process of **hygienic** care and cleaning of a dog. It "is an important part of dog care," Rheya says. According to Rheya, regular grooming helps to make sure that a dog is healthy and comfortable. "Depending on the breed, age, and health of the dog," she continues, "grooming can be required daily." Many breeds, however, require significantly less grooming than this.

Looking at the Words

Something that is **hygienic** is clean and will not cause disease.

A Yorkshire Terrier is a dog breed whose hair will continue to grow like a human's. This dog will need more regular grooming than a short-haired breed like a Labrador.

A dog breed is a group of closely related and visibly similar dogs. The many breeds of dogs that we know today—Labrador Retrievers, Yorkshire Terriers, and German Shepherds, being the three most popular examples in the United States—were developed through years of **breeding**. Labrador Retrievers, for example, get their name from the purpose for which they were originally bred. Retrievers are a kind of hunting dog, typically used when hunting for birds such as ducks and geese, which were bred to retrieve the birds once a hunter had shot them.

"Certain breeds require grooming almost constantly," Rheya says. Many dog breeds lose and re-grow hair year round in a process called shedding. Other breeds, such as Poodles, "molt" or lose their hair only once or twice a year. These kinds of breeds require grooming by a professional every six to eight weeks.

"How often you *have* to groom a dog," Rheya says, "depends on a lot. But no matter the circumstances, having your dog groomed will always be good for a dog's physical and emotional health."

According to Rheya, one reason owners have their dog groomed is to build a closer bond with their dog. "Bringing your dog to a groomer is one way to show that you care about your dog," Rheya says. The people who have the skills to best care for our dogs are known as "dog groomers"—and while grooming requires many skills and a lot of care, one thing that is *not* required is a college education!

Volunteering at a dog shelter is a great way to get experience with dogs.

The College Question

"When I was thinking about going to college," Rheya says, "a college education wasn't considered as important as it is today. College, then, was a way to get skills, not the only way to get skills."

As Rheya suggests, many people today do see college as the only way to find a stable, well-paying career. This is part of the reason that in

2011, nearly seven out of every ten students who graduated high school went on to attend college.

Unfortunately a college education isn't necessarily a safe bet when it comes to finding a successful career. According to CNN, the average student, in 2012, graduated college nearly $27,000 in debt. This much debt takes an average of ten years to pay off. CNN also reported that *half* of all college graduates could either not find a job or they found a job that didn't even require a college degree!

"I always loved animals," Rheya says, explaining how she originally became interested in grooming dogs. "Animals are wonderful," she continues, "especially dogs. They provide **unconditional** love. They don't care what you look like, how much money you make, what color your skin is, or what gender you are. All that dogs care about is whether or not you are kind to them."

While she was in high school, Rheya volunteered at local animal shelters. "This was much more than just getting experience," she says. "At the facility where I worked, we took dogs, puppies, cats, and kittens from shelters where they were about to be **euthanized**. We worked with them, played with them, taught them basic commands, cared for their needs, and if they were sick, we did our best to get them well so they could be sent to adoption centers to find loving homes. We worked very hard to make the animals adoptable, so they could give many years of love and loyalty to new owners."

This volunteer experience Rheya had during high school

> ## Looking at the Words
>
> **Unconditional** means without limits or requirements.
>
> When an animal is **euthanized**, it is killed peacefully and painlessly.

Do You Have a Passion?

There's a lot of talk about passion these days: "Find your passion... Pursue your passion... Do what you love..." But passion, it turns out, lives in all sorts of places. There is only one real formula: try things. Try things and see how they fit. Try jobs and find out what you like—and just as important, find out what you don't like. Passion can come later. Right now, just find something you enjoy. That's a starting point. Maybe it'll become that thing you can do for hours and it feels like only a few minutes have gone by. But don't put that pressure on yourself. Start small.

Adapted from the essay "The Truth About Finding Your Passion" by Colin Ryan. More of his work can be found at his website: http://astanduplife.com.

would shape the course of her professional life. It helped her see what she wanted to do with her life—and it showed her that a college education was not necessary for her to achieve her dreams.

High school is an influential time for most young people. Both in and out of their classes, young people have opportunities to explore their interests. Many students, by this time, are old enough to begin to

explore old hobbies more deeply or take on new ones. Rheya's time at the animal shelter, for example, allowed her to build on an interest she'd had since she was a young child. It gave her valuable knowledge for her future career and allowed her to grow her passion for working with and comforting animals.

"When you work with animals," she says, "you have to be extremely calm. They can sense if you are afraid and will bite or jump in order to defend themselves. Working with difficult dogs in the shelter was a great way to begin to learn how to be confident around aggressive or fearful dogs."

Even today, Rheya spends much of her free time volunteering at animal shelters and advocating for pet adoption agencies. "Only about 30 percent of cats and dogs are adopted from shelters or animal rescues," Rheya says. "Millions of dogs and cats a year are euthanized. Dogs and cats that are owned live longer healthier lives than strays or those in shelters. Animals love us and need love. That's why I still volunteer at shelters—and it's the same reason why I became a dog groomer."

For Rheya, a college education was not nearly as important as doing something that she loves. But doing what you love doesn't mean you necessarily need to settle for a smaller paycheck! According to the American Pet Products Association, Americans spent $50 billion on their pets in 2011. Spending in this area has increased each year since 2001. This means that there are growing opportunities for dog groomers like Rheya.

So should you go to college? It is an important question. There are a lot of options out there and one of the best decisions that anyone can make is to get educated about education. Ask yourself: "What do I love to do? What are my hobbies? What do I have a passion for? Do I need to go to college to get the skills that I need to be successful? How can I eventually earn a living doing what I love?"

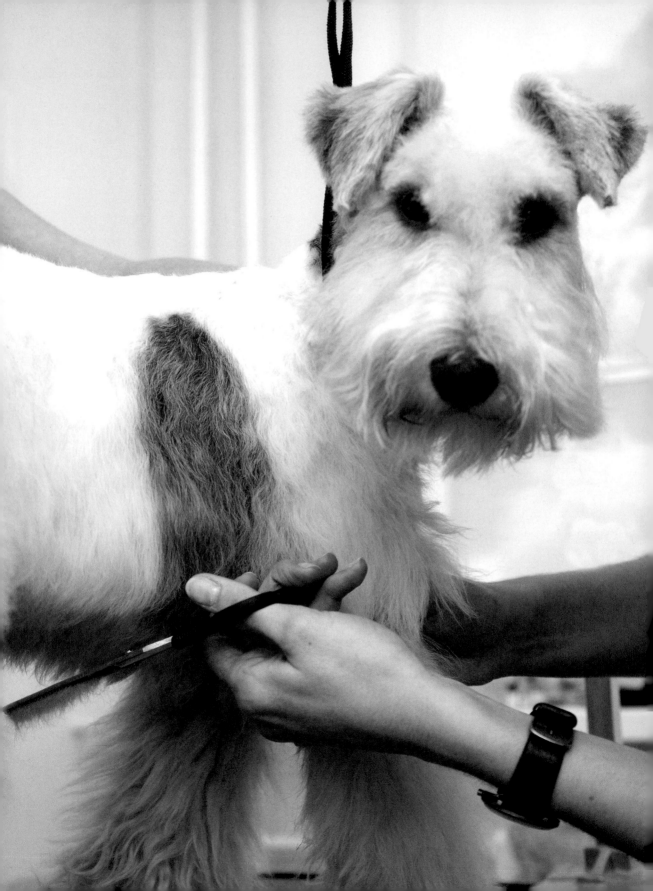

CHAPTER 2

What Do Dog Groomers Do?

According to Jan DeAngelo, there are many reasons to have your dog groomed. Jan has been grooming dogs for about eight years and works at a shop that specializes in creative grooming. Creative grooming is a style of dog grooming that's different from traditional grooming because it commonly involves artificial colors and non-traditional cuts. Making dogs look like other animals such as horses, giraffes, or pandas are some common creative cuts. Traditional dog grooming,

on the other hand, gives dogs one of a number of cuts considered appropriate for a specific breed of dog.

"I started working at this shop because I liked the freedom that creative grooming gives a groomer," Jan says, "but creative grooming is really only a small part of our business, since creative grooming defeats many of the practical reasons that someone would want or need to get their dogs groomed. Most clients come to us for traditional grooming and will occasionally get some pet tuning on holidays or special occasions." Pet tuning is a simpler form of creative grooming offered at usually a fraction of the cost of a creative cut. Pet tuning can be a great way for owners to have a hand in stylizing their dog and can build a stronger bond between a dog and owner.

The reasons to have a dog groomed include:

- decreased chances of various health problems such as **thrush**, scratches and other skin problems
- general cleanliness
- **monitoring** the dog's health by checking for cuts, heat, swelling, or changes in temperament, which could indicate illness
- building a closer bond between an owner and their dog

- reducing the chances of **infestation** by parasites such as fleas, ticks, or tapeworms

"Dogs are a part of the family," Jan says, "and grooming is good both for the owners and the dog." Grooming makes a dog more comfortable, happy, and healthy. "A clean dog is a dog that can be cuddled. Since dogs cannot talk, dogs and their owners communicate through other senses, such as touch." Not only does grooming make a dog a cleaner presence in their owner's home but it also protects the health of the human members of the family. Many of the kinds of parasites and diseases to which dogs are **susceptible** can be passed from dogs to humans.

Grooming a Dog

Dog grooming might sound like a simple job, but a lot of hard work is required to do even a traditional groom.

"A groomer is responsible for **customer service**, client relationships, and animal care, among other things," Jan says. "The most important job that a groomer is responsible for, though, is making sure that the dog remains safe while it is in your care. Customers can be a nightmare in any business, but I can't imagine anything worse than a customer whose dog was injured while in the care of a groomer."

According to Jan, before any groomer begins to groom a dog, she must deal with the customers. After a groomer meets the dog and owner, she has to find out how the owner wants the dog to look once groomed and

Looking at the Words

A **customer service** job involves helping people buy something from a business.

A groomer may use a brush like this to remove loose hair and knots from a dog's coat.

when the owner wants to pick up the dog. Inspecting the dog is also an important part of the **intake** process.

"Dogs, especially those that aren't groomed often," Jan says, "can come in with all sorts of issues that can affect the final grooming price. If they have fleas or mites, they will need to be washed

with a special flea shampoo. This can be expensive stuff and usually requires an additional fee. Having some on hand to sell to a customer is a good idea, but flea shampoo isn't meant to be a permanent solution for dogs. Fleas often live in the home. Educating customers about fleas gives them a chance to begin to take care of the issue before they bring the dog home."

According to Jan, another issue that should be addressed with a customer is "matting." Matted fur is too tangled to be combed out and restored, so it must be cut off and allowed to regrow. "Some customers really hate to hear that their dogs have matted fur. They'll try to refuse to have the matted fur cut off. Matted fur can be uncomfortable for a dog, though. Besides, matted fur is almost always dirty fur. Owners are better off having that fur removed from their pets. Groomers save themselves big headaches by going over issues like these before letting a customer leave. Customers don't like surprises!"

Once a groomer has determined what kind of cut he is giving a dog and if any other issues need to be addressed, he begins by pre-cutting the dog. This involves removing the excess or matted hair. Pre-cutting is important because it allows the shampoo to better penetrate a dog's skin.

After pre-cutting, a dog is bathed and dried. While bathing a dog, groomers will take care of removing any excess or shedding hair that wasn't removed during the pre-cut. They also clean the dog's ears and express the dog's anal glands. This is a technique that involves squeezing the glands located on either side of a dog's anus to release the contents. It is an important part of making sure that a dog is clean and comfortable.

"Some groomers prefer to cage dry a dog," Jan says, "in order to bathe or groom other dogs while the dog is drying. But I prefer to hand dry the dogs. Cage drying, depending on the breed and age of the dog, can be uncomfortable and even dangerous. Some dogs have died because the groomer got distracted with something else and left the dog in the cage drier too long." A cage dryer is a special kind of cage that uses a

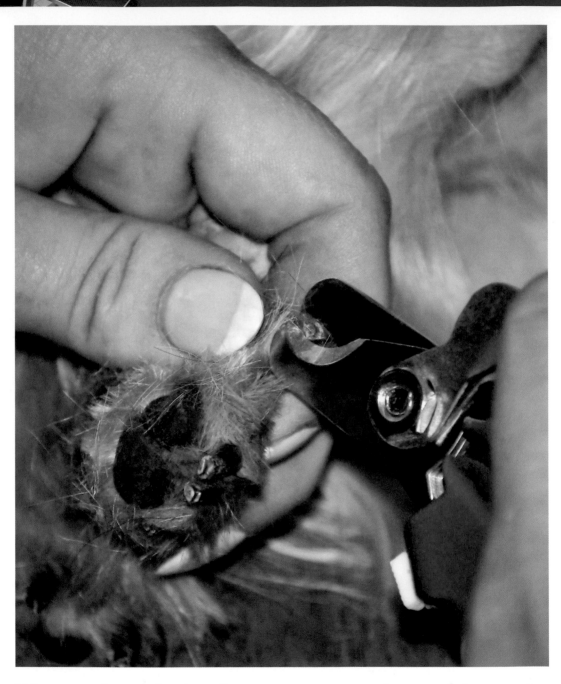

When cutting a dog's nails, a groomer must be careful not to injure the dog.

combination of heat and fans to dry a dog. There are many models available and some are considered more dangerous than others.

Once a dog is bathed and dried, the nails are cut and any other finishing touches are made. If the owner requests them, perfume, bows, or a bandana can be added. "At this point, the grooming has been completed," Jan says, "but the dogs must still be cared for. They will need to be given water, taken out for a short walk to use the bathroom, and then put into kennel or some other safe area to wait for their owners to pick them up."

Other Services and Responsibilities

While the bathing and grooming process makes up most of the work that a dog groomer is paid to do, there are other tasks and services dog groomers do that are either **optional** for a customer or required for the business. Grooming can be a very messy business, for example, and after a day of grooming is done, a groomer will need to sweep hair, wrap up cords, and sterilize tools so that they are ready for the next day.

"Don't forget," Jan says, "that in order to make enough money, a groomer will need to groom multiple dogs a day. If you're working alone, without any employees, this means you will need to answer phones, check-in and check-out dogs,

Looking at the Words

Something that is **optional** doesn't have to be done; it is not required.

Leashes, brushes, clippers, and plenty of treats are a groomer's most important tools.

Dog Tattoos

One dog-grooming fad that has recently developed is dog tattoos. Traditional tattoos (for humans) are permanent and are inked directly into the skin, but dog tattoos are air brushed onto a dog's fur using a stencil and a special pet-friendly dye. These tattoos come in a variety of formats and are used by owners who want to advertise a business, sports fans who want to show off their team allegiance, or pet owners who simply want to extend the gift of style to their four-legged companions.

and care for all of the other animals in the shop." Groomers need to be able to **multitask** in order to make it all work.

There are many other services that are commonly offered by dog groomers that can be great ways for groomers to make some extra money without doing much additional work. One of these services involves "kenneling" or allowing dogs to stay in your cages for an extended period of time while their owners are away.

"Most shops also sell some pet-care products," Jan says, "in order to make some extra money. What kinds of good you carry generally depends on who your clients are. Most shops carry dog treats, for example. Other shops, like mine, are located in big cities, which means we often have more clients than we can handle. So we sell

Looking at the Words

To **multitask** is to do many different things at once.

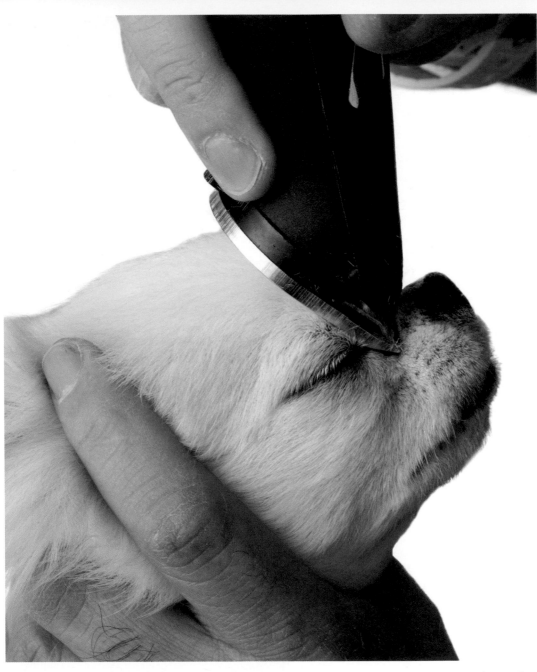

When trimming around a dog's eyes, it's very important that the groomer be able to keep the dog calm and quiet.

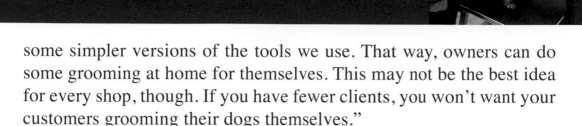

some simpler versions of the tools we use. That way, owners can do some grooming at home for themselves. This may not be the best idea for every shop, though. If you have fewer clients, you won't want your customers grooming their dogs themselves."

Dog groomers' most important responsibility, of course, is making sure that a dog remains comfortable and safe while in their care. "This is much harder than it sounds," Jan says. According to Jan, some dogs become very stressed when they are in the care of a groomer. "Bites can happen," he admits, "but a good groomer knows when a dog is feeling fear or anxiety. We can tell when dogs are about to become aggressive or react. That's really a vital skill to have. It wouldn't be such a problem if the groomer were the only one who could get hurt. I don't want to get bit, but I can cope with it. What's worse, though, is if a dog hurts itself. Like if a dog jumps when I have a pair of scissors in my hand, the dog can end up badly hurt. That's not something I want happening, ever. I'd much rather deal with my own blood than explain to an owner why her dog is bleeding!"

A dog groomer provides health, safety, and happiness to a dog and owner. The most successful groomers are the ones who truly care for each dog, even if that means a few nips from scared dogs and a few difficult customers now and then!

CHAPTER 3

How Can I Become a Dog Groomer?

"Dog grooming is a rewarding career," says Manuel Sandoval, a relatively new groomer with only a few years working in the field. "Grooming is a lot of hard work and there is a lot to learn. There are so many breeds that it takes a long time before you have groomed them all and get used to their all their different **temperaments** and personalities. For instance, Pugs and Greyhounds are easy to groom, and they have great

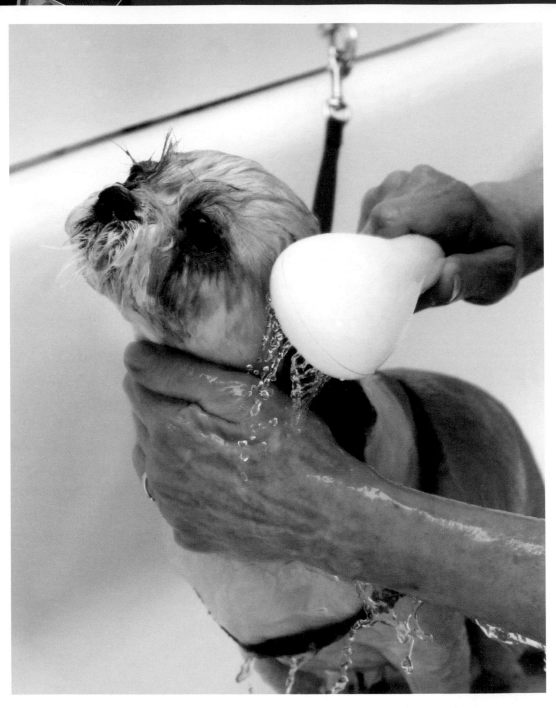

Being a dog groomer requires patience and gentleness.

DOG GROOMER

personalities. They do not get excited easily, and they are generally pretty obedient. But Shih Tzus and certain kinds of terriers are nightmares. They bark a lot and some of them are so small! A lot of time they shake almost constantly while they get groomed."

Luckily, a lot of the knowledge like this can be learned on the job. But before you pick up a pair of scissors and begin to work on a dog, you have many other skills you will need to learn.

What All Dog Groomers Need

According to Manuel, one of the best things about becoming a dog groomer is that you can try it out to see if it is a good fit for you. Since getting a job as a dog groomer doesn't take four years of college, you can give the profession a try and leave it if it is not the career for you.

"For a young person," Manuel says, "if you are deciding whether or not to go to college, I'd recommend you take a good look at yourself. I mean, what are your skills? What are you good at doing, really? And what do you like doing?"

Manuel makes an important point. Grooming dogs might sound like a lot of fun but not everyone is cut out for it. Maybe, for example, you like dogs—but the thought of pressing a dog's anal glands really grosses you out! But on the other hand, maybe once you get used to the idea and get some experience, you'll discover it's really not such a big deal for

you. One of the best ways to figure out what you want to do in life is to try different things now. That way you can see for yourself what you really like best. You might even surprise yourself!

Like Rheya from chapter 1, Manuel also began working with animals at a young age. "I volunteered at a vet's office when I was in high school," he says. "It was a great way to learn how to work with animals. I learned some simple grooming techniques there too. Vets do some of that too, so once I proved I could do it, the vet was happy to let me take care of any grooming they needed. But I think learning how to work with animals was the most important part. If you are calm then they will be calm. If you are too loud or you get excited easy, working with animals may not be right for you. Animals can sense what you feel."

According to Manuel, some classes in high school, like biology, for example, can offer some good knowledge that anyone working with animals should have. "I'm not a vet, and I don't pretend to be. But I use the stuff I learned in high school to help me understand a dog's body better. I do some reading too, whenever I can. It just helps me be the best I can. And I'm really interested."

The Bureau of Labor Statistics lists six traits that anyone working with animals should have:

- **Compassion.** All workers must be **compassionate** when dealing with animals and their owners. They should genuinely like animals and treat them with kindness.
- **Customer-service skills.** Animal-care workers should understand pet owners' needs so they can provide services that leave the owners satisfied. Some animal-care workers may need to deal with upset pet owners.
- **Detail oriented.** Workers must be **detail oriented** because they are often responsible for maintaining records and monitoring changes in animals' behavior.

- **Patience.** Animal caretakers need to be patient when dealing with animals that do not respond to commands.
- **Problem-solving skills.** Animal caretakers must have problem-solving skills when dealing with animal behaviors. They must assess whether the animals are responding to their methods and identify which methods are most successful.
- **Stamina. Stamina** is important for animal-care workers because their work often involves kneeling, crawling, bending, and, occasionally, lifting heavy animals and supplies.

According to Manuel, these are all skills that he uses daily, but patience is by far the most important skill to have. "If you are patient," he says, "then a scared or excited dog will likely calm down. Then you are less likely to make mistakes. Also, certain breeds have long coats, which need a lot of work and patience. If you are impatient while you work, the dog senses it. That isn't good for either you or the dog."

Examine yourself and be honest. If you already have some of these skills, then you are well on your way to an exciting life as a dog groomer. If you are not very strong in some of these areas, then now is the time to begin to practice these skills. They'll serve you well in other careers besides dog grooming!

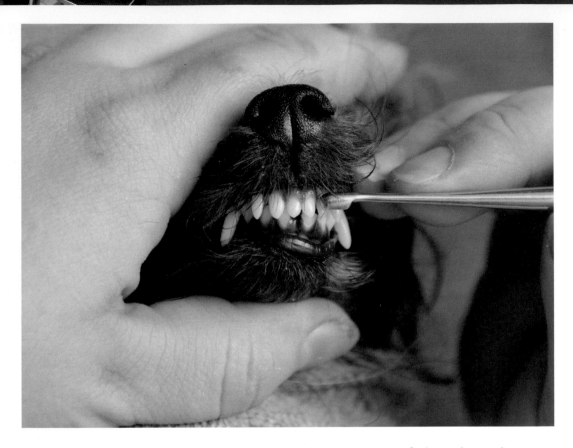

Cleaning a dog's teeth can be a challenging if the dog doesn't want to cooperate!

Becoming a Dog Groomer

"Becoming a groomer is a pretty simple process," Manuel says. "The most difficult part is finding training." While the law does not regulate

dog groomers and no **certification** is needed to become a groomer, it is still absolutely necessary to get training. "If you just open up a shop without knowing what you're doing," Manuel comments, "your customers will figure out pretty quick. Your business won't last long."

One of the most popular ways to learn how to groom dogs is to become an **apprentice** of a **veteran** groomer. According to Manuel, some groomers will allow you to pay them for training as an apprentice. The price and length of the training typically depends on how much experience the groomer has. According to the Bureau of Labor Statistics, most grooming apprenticeships last between twelve and twenty weeks.

While paying for apprenticeship is one way to get training, Manuel says that he didn't have to pay for his training at all. "The shop that I began working at needed an extra pair of hands. So I asked if I could be trained while I worked a job for free." Manuel began his career washing dogs in the shop where he was working, and he received training instead of a paycheck. "Some people I know," Manuel says, "even found paid apprenticeships. They got a small paycheck for the work they did—and they got all of the training they need at the same time."

Other options include going to a grooming school or taking classes in grooming online. Most programs such as these end in a certification

Looking at the Words

Certification is a formal, written assurance that a person is capable of doing a job.

A person who is an **apprentice** is training for a specific job by doing that job.

A **veteran** is someone who has had a lot of experience in a certain job.

The Pooch Parlor, a grooming school licensed through the Idaho Board of Education, offers training to students that come from all over the nation to acquire certification (www.poochparlor.net).

from the National Dog Groomers Association of America (NDGAA). According to Manuel, these school and online classes can be good, but they sometimes offer little hands-on training, so they should be combined with other experiences. Certification by the NDGAA involves two tests, one that is written and one that demonstrates a groomer's practical skills. Demonstrating your practical skills requires grooming four different breeds, one from each of the four major kinds of breeds: sporting, non-sporting, short-legged terriers, and long-legged terriers. Certification can be a way to prove to employers that you have the skills you need to begin a career as a groomer and be able to **negotiate** better wage. But, according to Manuel, some schools like this can be expensive—and certification is not required to be successful as a groomer.

Many pet corporations that offer grooming services, such as Petco, offer a combination of hands-on experience and classroom education when training new groomers. Manuel warns, however, that the other two options should be explored first before seeking training from a corporate store. "Large pet stores kind of have a bad reputation. That means getting employed anywhere else can be difficult if this is where you were trained."

No matter how you get the skills you need, though, compared to a college education, the small investment of time and money means you could soon be qualified for an exciting career as a dog groomer!

How Can I Become a Dog Groomer?   **39**

CHAPTER 4

How Much
Can I Make?

Because the majority of dog groomers in America are self-employed, it can be very difficult to say how much money the average dog groomer makes a year. (To be self-employed means that you are not paid regular wages by an employer, but instead, you work for yourself.)

"Multiple dog groomers might work at a single dog-grooming business," says Hannah Singleton, "but most or all of them will be considered self-employed because most dog

Dog groomers who are actually hair stylists may make more money.

DOG GROOMER

groomers work for commissions." This means they are paid a certain percentage of every groom that they complete. Hannah is the owner of a dog-grooming business; she says she has been working as a groomer for "at least fifteen years now."

According to Hannah, there are positives and negatives about being self-employed. On the one hand, being self-employed allows a groomer to set her own working hours, and it gives a groomer some control over how much she charges for grooming. On the other hand, being self-employed means that a regular income is not guaranteed, and that certain benefits, such as health insurance, which would usually be paid for in full or in part by an employer, need to be paid for by the self-employed person.

"At my shop," Hannah says, "I offer an hourly wage to all the groomers who work with me. On top of that, I give all groomers 50 percent of whatever they make grooming. This means that groomers who work for me are not technically self-employed but they get the benefits of being self-employed. At the same time, they know they will definitely get a paycheck even during a slow week. I think my shop is rare, though. Anyone thinking of getting into the business should understand that they'll be working mostly off commissions. Unless they open their own business, of course."

High-Level Earnings

Dog groomers who own their own grooming business, like Hannah, have the potential to make very good money. Hannah not only owns the business, but she also works as a groomer. This means that for every groom she completes, she is able to keep 100 percent of the profits.

"Because of the way I pay the other groomers in the shop," Hannah says, "I make slightly less money than I would otherwise. But we

HAPPY DOG

CARING FOR YOUR DOG'S BODY, MIND AND SPIRIT

Billy Rafferty is one of the most successful dog groomers in the world.

Dog Groomer for the Stars

Billy Rafferty, the owner of Doggy Dooz, a grooming shop in Chicago, and the co-author of *Happy Dog: Caring for Your Dog's Body, Mind, and Spirit*, has perhaps the most glamorous dog-grooming job in the world. He is the personal groomer of Oprah Winfrey's dogs, and, as of July 2010, had a waiting list of over 300 clients. According to Rafferty, practice, patience, and an absolute love of animals set him apart from other groomers and earned him a reputation as "groomer to the stars."

are a good business, so we are usually booked solid almost the whole year round. I'm pretty sure that whatever I lose from my own income is gained back because of the fact that my groomers are happy." According to Hannah, happy groomers means happy animals—and happy animals means happy owners. Happy owners come back more often and are more likely to tip.

"Tips," Hannah says, "are a pretty big part of dog grooming. They are usually not factored in when people talk about how much they make a year." A fast groomer can finish up to about nine grooms a day and, according to Hannah, about 80 percent of her customers tip. "My regulars tip almost every time," she says. By "regulars," Hannah means repeat customers who are happy with the service she provides.

So what does all that mean? If Hannah charges on average $20 for each grooming, she could make $180 a day just from the dogs she

The owner of this shop caters to many dog owners' needs, from treats to daycare to grooming.

grooms herself. Then you add on to that the tips she makes, which could be another $35 or more. Now she's earning $210 a day—or as much as $1050 a week! And that doesn't include the money she gets from her employees jobs.

The Bureau of Labor Statistics lists customer-service skills as an important skill for any dog groomer to have and,

as Hannah suggests, good customer-service skills will lead to more money and more tips.

Being a business owner means that you control just about every aspect of your business. Having this much control is a lot of responsibility, but it also means that an owner can **strategize** to make the most money possible. According to Hannah, she uses a few different methods to bring in as much money as possible. Hannah's shop offers regular discounts, for example, and has special discounts for repeat customers. "For owners of small dogs," Hannah says, "we offer a weekly bath for only $10. Other shops offer monthly baths for usually about $25, but monthly baths can be a lot of work, because the dogs are so dirty after a month. Signing customers up for weekly baths means that we make $40 a dog rather than $25, and we also give customers more chances to tip us for doing a good job." Hannah's shop offers "spa treatments" and small extras as well, such as brushing a dog's teeth. These bonuses do not require much extra work but can bring in a lot of extra money.

Hannah also uses her store space to sell **retail** items such as shampoos, dog vitamins, dog treats, and collars. She lets local retails sell the items out of her shop, and she keeps part of the profit that she makes for

If a dog is going to be in dog shows, very specific cuts may be required, such as this standard poodle's.

each sale. Selling items this ways means that she makes more money without having to do any extra work and without having to buy the items to stock her shelves. Though sales are not always good, there is no risk involved for her, so even only a few sales a month will still add money to her income.

"Being a business owner is about being strategic," Hannah says— and any strategic business owner can make the kind of money that Hannah makes. According to her, the average incomes of grooming business owners are around $40,000 a year after rent and taxes are paid. Hannah makes, on average, about $50,000 a year after she pays all of her expenses. "I've had some good years, though," she says, "when I've made over $65,000!"

Average Salaries

Part of Hannah's success is due to her having chosen a good location for her business. Her shop is located in Westchester, New York, a highly populated suburb of New York City. "I originally thought of setting up a shop in New York City itself," Hannah says, "because there are a lot of dogs in New York." Hannah eventually, however, decided to establish her business in Westchester because the price of rent is significantly cheaper compared to New York City, and its location still offered her a large number of clients. Many of those clients also have high incomes, which means that they can afford to pay to have their pets groomed.

Not all dog groomers, however, will have the ability to establish a shop in an area like this. Likewise, most dog groomers do not have the kind of experience needed to open a shop and understand all that is needed to make their shops as successful as Hannah's.

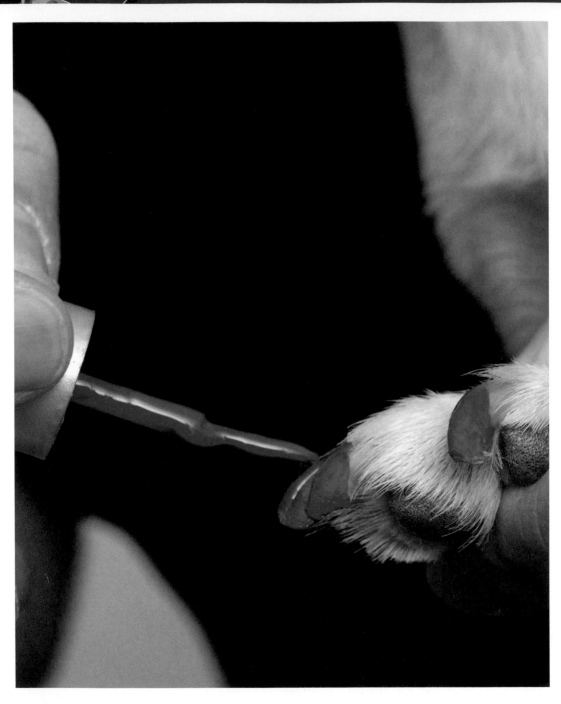

Applying polish to a dog's toenails takes a steady hand!

According to the Bureau of Labor Statistics, the average non-farm animal caretaker (of which dog groomers are a part) makes nearly $20,000 a year—but when you consider that 35 percent of all nonfarm animal caretakers work part time, the average salary of a full-time dog groomer is significantly higher than this. According to Payscale.com, for example, the average dog groomer in 2013 makes nearly $28,000 a year, close to the average for all careers, even those that require a college education!

CHAPTER 5

Looking to the Future

I f you are interested in pursuing dog grooming as a career, then you need to know what the future of the dog-grooming industry is looking like. Luckily, due to the increasing number of homes with pets, dog groomers will continue to be in high demand for years to come.

According to DegreeDirectory.com, for example, between 2008 and 2018, the number of dog groomers is expected to grow by 21 percent. The Bureau of Labor Statistics

lists a similar number, predicting that the number of non-farm and animal caretakers, of which dog groomers are a part, are expected to grow by 28 percent between 2010 and 2020, which is about double the growth expected for all careers in the United States during the same period. A growing demand for dog groomers will also lead to higher salaries for talented groomers.

While the future of dog groomers certainly looks bright, there are some laws being considered by states that could make becoming a dog groomer more difficult. In 2012, for example, California considered but did not pass a bill that would ask all existing and **prospective** dog groomers to become voluntarily certified and would subject grooming shops to **random** inspections throughout the year. No states have passed bills like this, but they have been proposed in numerous states so far.

In general dog groomers are split over the need for bills like this. On the one hand, dogs have been hurt and in some very rare instances killed by **irresponsible** groomers. Similarly, some groomers operating today are not qualified to be grooming dogs or handling animals, and yet they are allowed to operate due to the lack of regulation. On the other hand,

the large growth of the industry could potentially be **stifled**. Some people argue that regulations like this wouldn't necessarily make grooming safer for the pets, since most groomers who have injured animals would have been certified by the standards that the bill called for.

If you open a shop similar to this one, you may make a lot more money—but you will also have a lot more responsibilities.

Few Chances for Advancement

Looking at the Words

An **advancement** is a promotion or an improvement.

Finance is the way money is managed by an individual or a business.

Bookkeeping is how people keep track of a business's money. Bookkeeping is also called accounting.

Expenditures are money spent to run a business.

Someone who is **passionate** has a great love for what they are doing.

Advancement as a dog groomer is available but limited. Making more money will always be available to groomers who are willing to open their own dog grooming businesses. Becoming a business owner, however, can be a lot of responsibility and stress that may not be worth the extra money for some people.

As we discussed in chapter 4, opening a successful business is also dependent on where a groomer lives. One grooming business may be more than enough for a small rural town. A city, on the other hand, will offer plenty of chances to open grooming businesses—but at the same time, the cost of living and working in many cities can be staggering. Similarly, a city will likely have more grooming businesses with which a starting business must compete.

Many skills and years of experience will likely be needed before someone is ready to open his own shop. To be a successful business owner, you need to master the basics of **finance** and organization. You need to be able to do basic **bookkeeping** on income and **expenditures**. You'll need to know about the tax and business laws that apply to your business, and you'll need to organize insurance, pay bills and track invoices.

Groomers can learn many business skills in order to bring themselves more money and more success. Some groomers, like Jan from chapter 2, learn how to groom creatively. He is part of the National Association of Professional Creative Groomers (NAPCG), which holds annual contests for creative groomers where they can show off their grooming masterpieces and earn fame for their grooming abilities. Being able to prove your skill to your customers will give them a reason to come back and a reason to pay more money for your services. So while "advancement" might not be available to dog groomers in the same way it is in other career paths, that is no reason for groomers to ever stop learning and developing their skills. The more skills you have—whatever your career—the more valuable your services will be!

Conclusion

The people interviewed in this book are intelligent, driven, and **passionate** about what they are doing. They all had the willingness to adventure and learn, even if learning didn't mean sitting in a classroom. More important, for each of them, success didn't only mean the amount of money earned. For all of these dog groomers, success means pursuing what they are passionate about; it means learning all they can about themselves and their interests; it means defining their own standards of success.

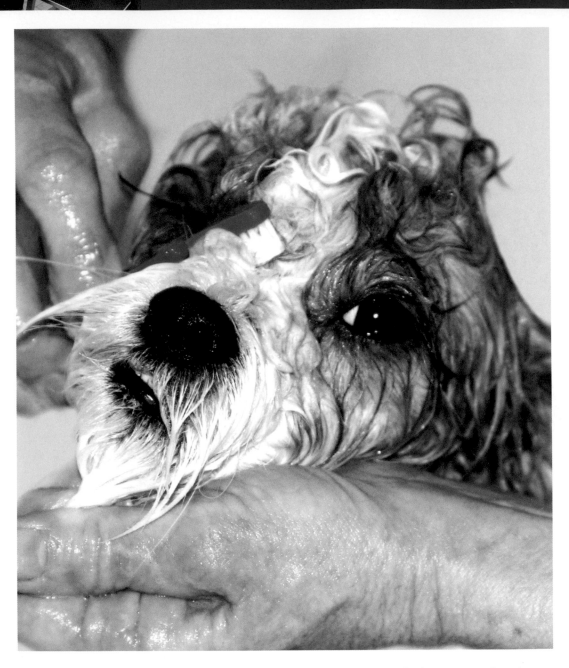

Do you love dogs? Do you love being around them and taking care of them? If so, a career as a dog groomer might be one of the many possibilities you want to consider.

For many people, college is the perfect choice and an important learning experience. Not only can it open the doors of certain careers but it is also often the first experience that many young people have at living away from home without the safety and security of their parents. This is a great learning experience.

Unfortunately, many students go to college with no clear idea how to use the college experience to connect them with a lifetime of success. In some cases, young people go to college only because they felt pressured do so by their peers or their parents. Many students leave college still with no idea of what they want from a career. And because of the staggering debt that many students have to acquire just to go to college, they may be in a far worse financial position than before.

What does success mean to you? Does it mean the amount of money you make? Or does it mean spending the majority of your time doing something you enjoy, something that makes you feel fulfilled and excited about your life? What do you most enjoy doing in life? What interests you?

There is no single right answer to these questions. The "right answer" for you will be based on honesty and a willingness to learn. Take advantage of every learning opportunity that comes your way, both in school and out of school. Learn as much as you can from your classes and schoolbooks, but also talk to your teachers. Pick their brains about their own experiences. Talk to your guidance counselor. Talk to other adults in your life. Read books in a variety of topics. Even fiction can give you a good idea what various jobs might be like. Check out jobs on the Internet too. Volunteer in various ways. Be open to new ideas about both yourself and the world around you. Don't hesitate to try something new.

It's a big world out there, full of possibilities. Be willing to learn and work hard, no matter where life takes you!

Find Out More

In Books

Fernandez, Amy and Isabelle Francais. *Puppies: A Complete Guide to Caring for Your Puppy (Complete Care Made Easy)*. Irvine, Calif.: BowTie Press, 2011.

Haynes, Gaile F. *The Winning Team: A Guidebook for Junior Showmanship*. Wenatchee, Wash.: Dogwise Publishing, 2004.

Stone, Ben and Pearl Stone. *The Stone Guide to Dog Grooming For All Breeds*. Somerset, UK: Howell Book House, 2001.

On the Internet

Dog Breed Info Center
www.dogbreedinfo.com

How to Become a Dog Groomer
www.doggroomeradvice.com

National Dog Groomers Association for Professional Pet Groomers
www.nationaldoggroomers.com

Bibliography

"Animal Care and Service Workers." U.S. Bureau of Labor Statistics. http://www.bls.gov/ooh/personal-care-and-service/animal-care-and-service-workers.htm (accessed March 27, 2013).

Botos, Sue. "Work Is Shear Delight for Dog Groomer to the Stars." 2 Press Papers, July 30, 2010. http://2presspapers.northcoastnow.com/work-is-shear-delight-for-dog-groomer-to-the-stars/ (accessed March 28, 2013).

"Despite Economy, Most Still Willing to Spend Money on Pets." WBIR, October 11, 2011. http://www.wbir.com/news/article/187444/173/Despite-economy-most-still-willing-to-spend-money-on-pets (accessed March 28, 2013).

"Dog Groomer Hourly Rate." PayScale.com.http://www.payscale.com/research/US/Job=Dog_Groomer/Hourly Rate (accessed March 29, 2013).

"How Many Pets Are in the U.S.?" Netscape Home & Living. http://webcenters.netscape.compuserve.com/homerealestate/feature.jsp?story=rainingcatsanddogs (accessed March 28, 2013).

"Learn How to Become a Dog Groomer." How to Become a Dog Groomer. http://doggroomeradvice.com/ (accessed March 27, 2013).

"Pet Statistics." ASPCA. http://www.aspca.org/about-us/faq/
pet-statistics.aspx (accessed March 27, 2013).

Power, Emma. "Furry Families: Making a Human-Dog Family
Through Home. Social and Cultural Geography, 2008 Aug; 9(5):535–
555. http://www.petpartners.org/document.doc?id=40 (accessed March
26, 2013).

Index

About the Author

Christie Marlowe lives in Binghamton, New York, where she works as a writer and web designer. She has a degree in literature, cares strongly about the environment, and spends three or more nights a week wailing on her Telecaster.

Picture Credits